Moving *from* Mexico

by Liz Rawlings

illustrated by Antonio Vincenti

Chapter 1

Chaos in Mexico City

José was 10, but Maria, his mother, said it was too dangerous these days for him to walk to school on his own. His father, Diego, took him today. José held one of his father's hands. His sister Ana, who was eight, held the other. They wove a path among angry people on the streets. José felt they were being herded like sheep. He missed being able to walk to school with just his sister. They used to race each other to see who could get to school first.

TEXTILE

At dinner that night, the family talked about what was happening in Mexico.

"When will we be able to walk to school by ourselves again?" Ana asked.

"I thought things were going to be better now that President Díaz resigned," added José.

José's mother explained that people were fighting over who would lead the country next.

"I'm afraid the country will be at war for some time," Diego said. "I've been thinking that we should move to California."

José was surprised. "But why, Dad?" he asked.

"The government won't be building any bridges or roads," Diego said. "It will be hard to find work."

"There might be more opportunities in California," said Maria. "They need engineers like your father to work on the new railroad."

Maria's words sounded positive, but she looked sad. José and Ana just looked at each other.

The next day at school, Ana looked around her class. She thought about the friends she would miss if they left Mexico. She had heard another girl talking about California, so she went over to her at lunchtime.

"Is your family moving to California?" she asked.

The other girl replied, "My dad thinks we would be safer there."

"Are you excited?" Ana asked.

"A bit—but I'm a bit scared, too."

That night, Ana told her family about her classmate.

Her father said, "Many people are leaving. I'm beginning to think that the sooner we get out, the better."

Chapter 2

Making the Move

The next month, Maria and Diego announced that the family was moving to California. Maria told José and Ana that they could only take things that were useful or valuable.

José was very excited. He was also nervous about going such a long way from home. José packed some clothes, but he made sure he had room for his model train and his guitar.

Ana sadly put all her dresses and some of her treasures in her suitcase. As she packed her favorite doll, she whispered to her, "Don't be scared. I'll take care of you."

When she was in bed, Ana heard gunshots and men shouting in the street. She pulled the blankets over her head to mask the noise.

The trip to California was long. First, the family had to travel by horse and carriage to the coast. It took several days, and it was not fun. The seats were hard, and the road was bumpy. José and Ana were bored and grumpy.

The steamer trip along the Gulf of California was a different matter. José and Ana had never seen the ocean before, let alone been on a ship. José loved spotting turtles, whales, and porpoises. Ana was excited when a pod of dolphins began leaping into the air in front of the boat.

When the ship docked, the family took another carriage ride to reach the border. The guards inspected their papers carefully, then waved them through. They were in California!

Chapter 3

A New School

The family moved into an apartment. Everything felt strange at first. José and Ana were nervous about starting at a new school. They both spoke English, but they were worried that people might not understand them.

José was surprised and happy to find that some of his classmates spoke Spanish. They came from Mexico, too. Their dads worked on the railroads or in factories. At break times, the Mexican children chatted together in Spanish.

Ana found it harder to settle than José did. She could chat easily in English but she found it hard to write. Sometimes she just doodled in the margin of her writing book. One day, her teacher came over with some paints and canvas.

"Why don't you paint a picture of Mexico City? It will help to remind you of home," she suggested.

Ana looked up shyly at her teacher. She thought for a moment, then she began to work on her painting.

Sometimes, José and Ana went with Maria to the market. They tried asking for things in English. They worked out the change in cents. Ana was happy that they could get her favorite chili peppers in California.

Maria bought pieces of brightly colored cloth at the market. She said it reminded her of home.

Chapter 4

Fun at the Beach

One Sunday, Ana gave her mother a present. It was a painting of their house in Mexico. Maria put it up on the wall. She chose a place next to the fireplace in the kitchen, where she could look at it often. The painting hung next to some photographs of Maria's sisters and brothers. She told Ana that the painting made her feel less homesick.

Later that day, the family packed a picnic and walked to the beach. They sat on mats under palm trees to eat their lunch.

After lunch, José and Ana ran out to the sea. They were learning to swim, but most of the time they just splashed like birds in the shallows.

As José and Ana played in the water, their parents watched them. Ana had lost the sad look she had when they arrived. She had made some friends. José had taken his guitar to school and was teaching his classmates some Mexican songs.

Diego and Maria smiled at each other. They were glad they had decided to immigrate.

When José and Ana came out of the water, they lay down on their beach towels. José said he felt as hot as an oven and asked if they could buy ice cream sodas. Diego reached into his pocket to pull out some change.

José grabbed it and said to Ana, "Race you to the store!"

Respond to Reading

Summarize

Use details from the text to summarize the events in the story *Moving from Mexico* and think about how they help you find the theme.

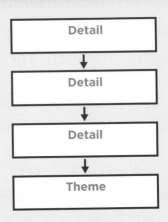

Text Evidence

1. How do you know *Moving from Mexico* is set in the past? GENRE

2. How do Ana's feelings about moving change during the story? Use details from the story to support your answer. THEME

3. What did the author mean when she said the children "splashed like birds"? SIMILE

4. In your own words, write about why the family in *Moving from Mexico* decided to go to the United States. WRITE ABOUT READING

Compare Texts

Read about the revolution that caused the family to leave Mexico and immigrate to America.

MEXICAN REVOLUTION
1910–1920

The Mexican Revolution began in 1910. At that time, the President of Mexico was Porfirio Díaz. Díaz ruled Mexico for 30 years. He fixed the elections so that he always won. Some people got very rich while Díaz was in power. Farmers and factory workers were very poor. In 1910, the average life span in Mexico City was only 24!

Mexicans wanted to improve things for everyone. They knew they would have to fight for this. Díaz resigned in 1911. However, the new leader, Francisco Madero, could not stop civil war from breaking out.

The battle cry of the revolution was "land and freedom." In the past, the rich were able to take land from poor farmers. The farmers wanted this to stop. The leader of the farmers was Emiliano Zapata. Zapata came from a poor farming family.

In 1914, peasant armies led by Zapata and his ally, Francisco Villa, marched into Mexico City. They demanded that land should be returned to the farmers.

Emiliano Zapata became a hero in Mexico during the revolution.

In 1917, Venustiano Carranza became president. He put in place a constitution that was the basis of Mexican democracy. The constitution provided for free education and workers' rights. It allowed for rural land to be given to the poor. In 1920, Alvaro Obregon was elected president. He set up schools and workers' unions. The election of Obregon meant the end of the revolution.

After the revolution had ended, artists painted murals on official buildings that told the story of the revolution. They used art to show Mexicans' new pride in their nation.

Make Connections

How does *Mexican Revolution* help you to understand *Moving from Mexico*?
ESSENTIAL QUESTION

Describe the difference in writing style between *Moving from Mexico* and *Mexican Revolution*.
TEXT TO TEXT

Focus on Genre

Historical Fiction *Moving from Mexico* is historical fiction. This kind of fiction tells a story that is set in the past. Although the characters are usually made up, the setting is real. Sometimes, some of the characters are also real historical people.

Read and Find *Moving from Mexico* is based on an historical event—the Mexican Revolution of 1910–1920. However, the main characters in the story are imaginary.

Your Turn

Think about an historical period you are interested in. Research what was happening at the time. Write your own story about an event that happened, peopling your story with imaginary characters.